NOTE-FOR-NOTE
KEYBOARD
TRANSCRIPTIONS

THE *Carole King*
KEYBOARD BOOK

Cover photo © 1993 Catherine Wessel
Photo courtesy of CK Productions
www.CaroleKing.com

ISBN 0-634-04549-0

In Australia Contact:
Hal Leonard Australia Pty. Ltd.
22 Taunton Drive P.O. Box 5130
Cheltenham East, 3192 Victoria, Australia
Email: ausadmin@halleonard.com

HAL•LEONARD®
CORPORATION
7777 W. BLUEMOUND RD. P.O. BOX 13819 MILWAUKEE, WI 53213

Visit Hal Leonard Online at
www.halleonard.com

ABOUT THIS BOOK

When playing through the transcriptions in this book, it is important to consider the following:

1. The primary keyboard part always appears directly below the vocal line.

2. Any secondary keyboard parts appear below the primary keyboard part. The instrument sound is always indicated in the measure in which the part is first played. (Sound changes are also indicated where appropriate.)

3. Other prominent instrumental parts, such as string and horn lines, are also included. It is important to note that these parts are arranged so that they may be played as secondary keyboard parts. The pitches are accurate; however, the voicings of the chords may be modified to be more indicative of a keyboard approach.

4. If there is no keyboard part on the recording for an extended time, other instrumental parts are often arranged to be played by the primary keyboard part. These sections are optional and are intended to be played only if the actual instruments (such as guitar) are not available.

5. "Fill" boxes are sometimes included when a particular fill, or figure, is played on the repeat or D.S. only. A typical indication would be "Play Fill 1 (2nd time)."

The transcriptions in this book are useful in a variety of situations: with a band, with a sequencer, with a CD, or solo playing. Whatever your purpose, you can now play your favorite songs just as the artists recorded them.

THE *Carole King* KEYBOARD BOOK

Contents

Beautiful

Words and Music by Carole King

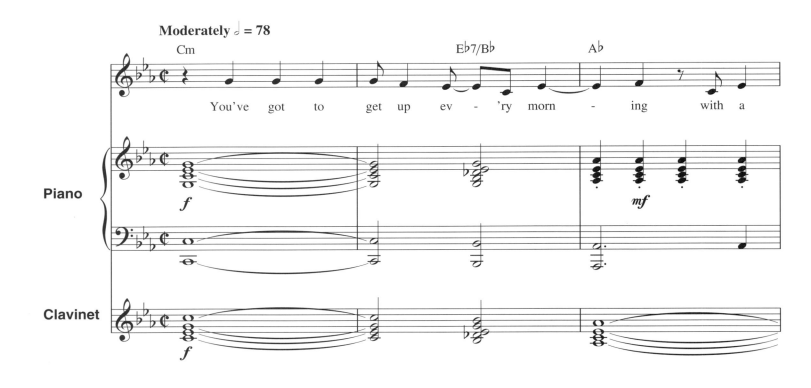

You've got to get up ev-'ry morn - ing with a

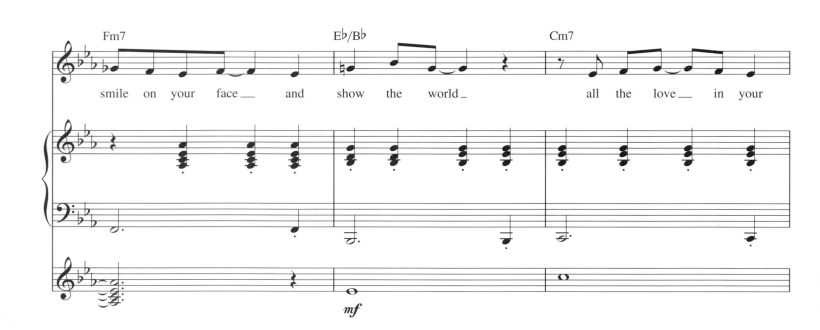

smile on your face __ and show the world __ all the love __ in your

5

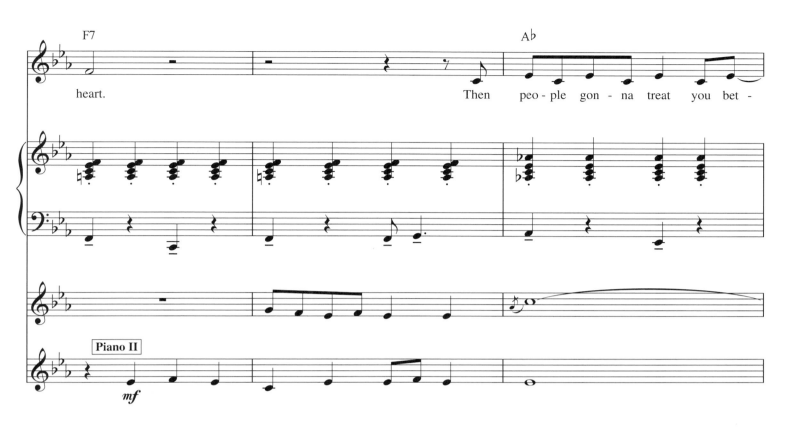

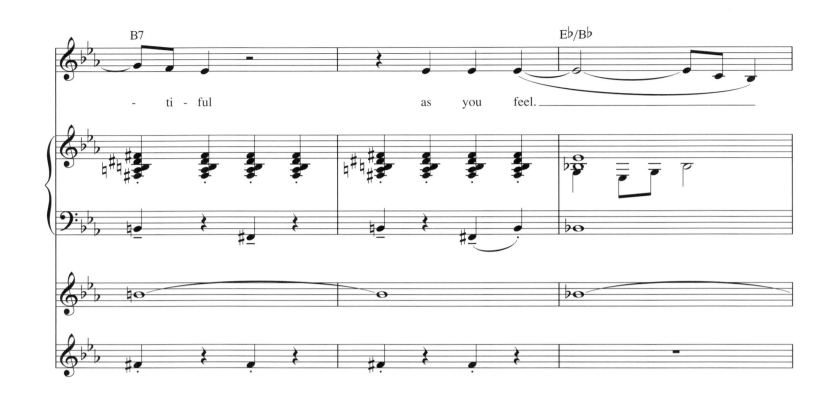

- ti - ful   as   you   feel. _____

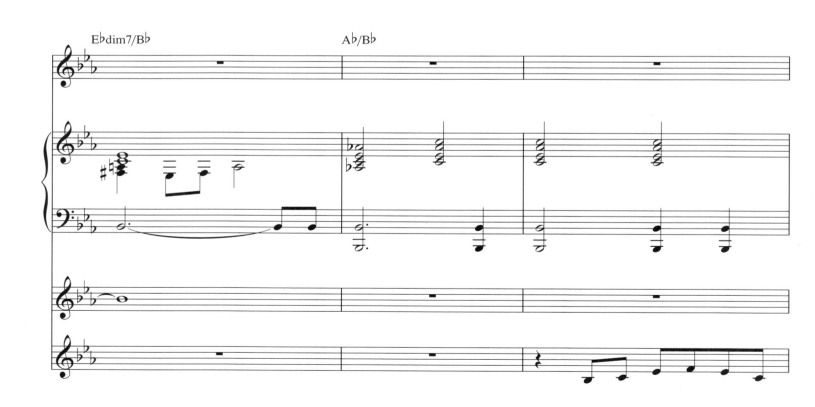

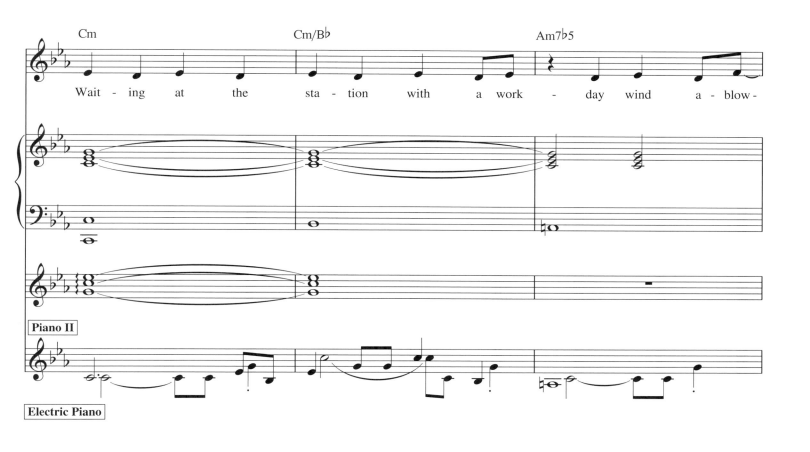

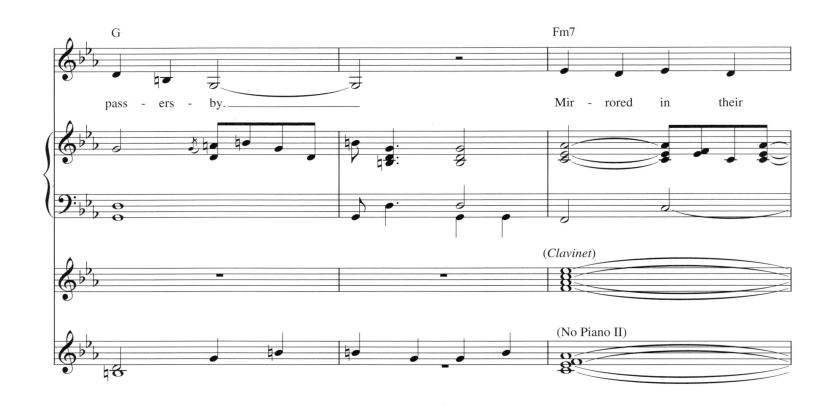

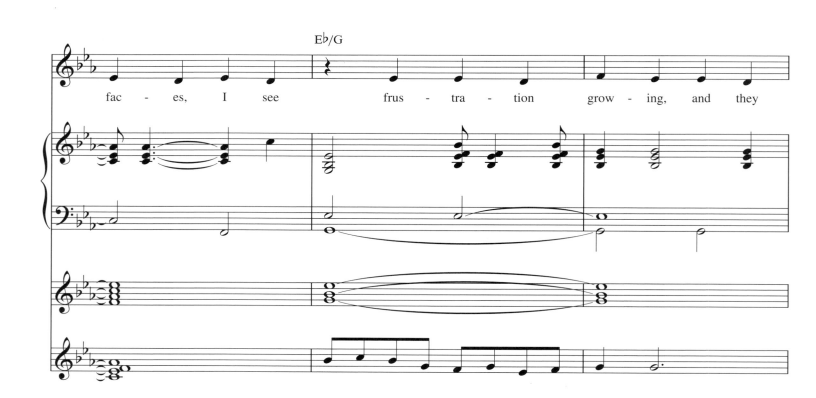

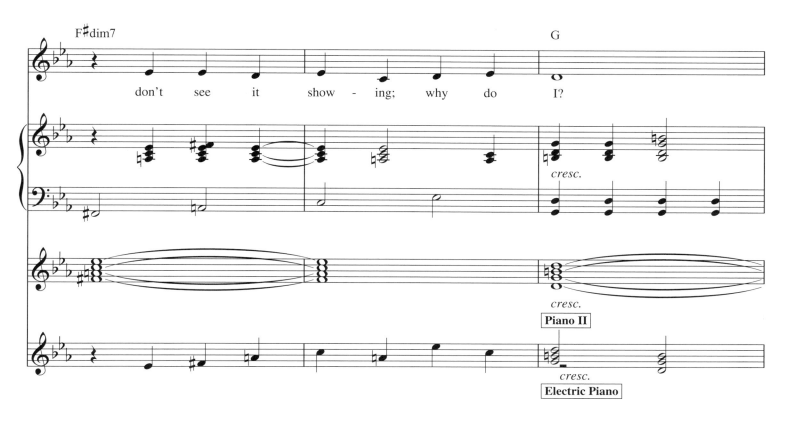

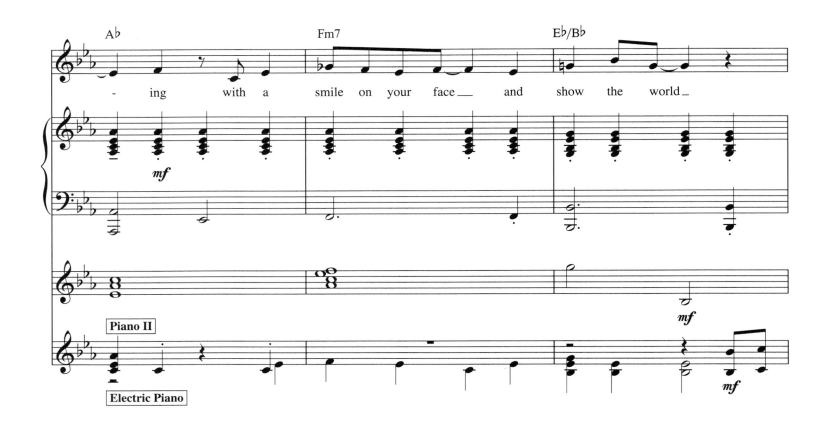

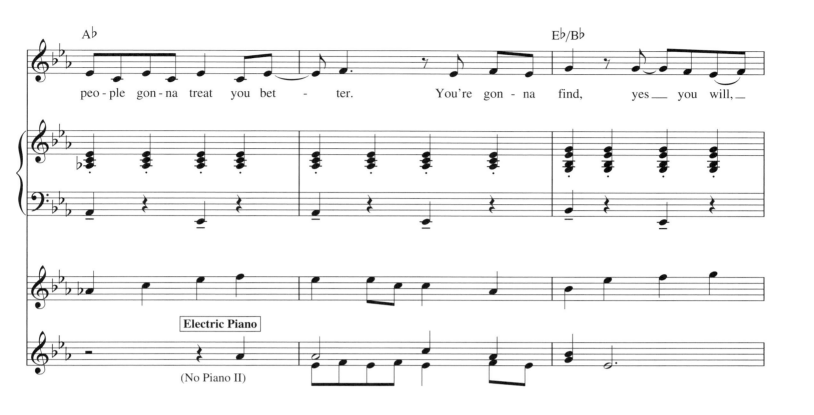

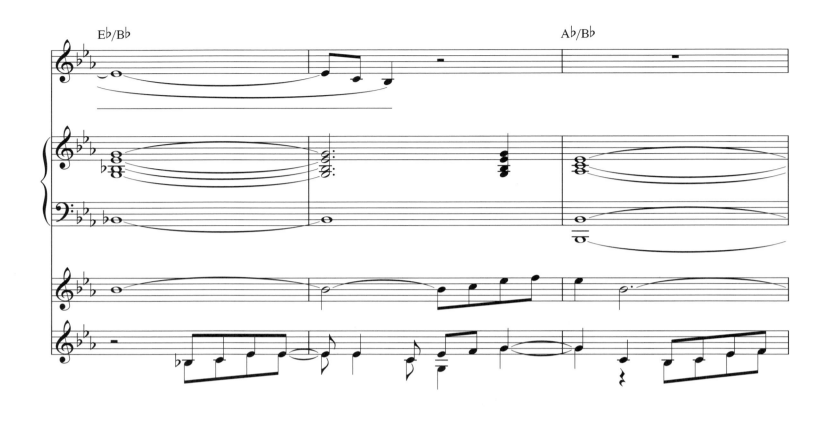

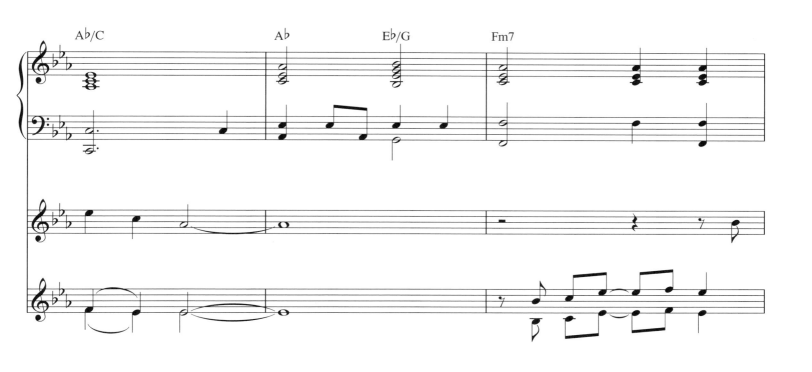

I have of-ten asked my - self the rea - son for the sad -

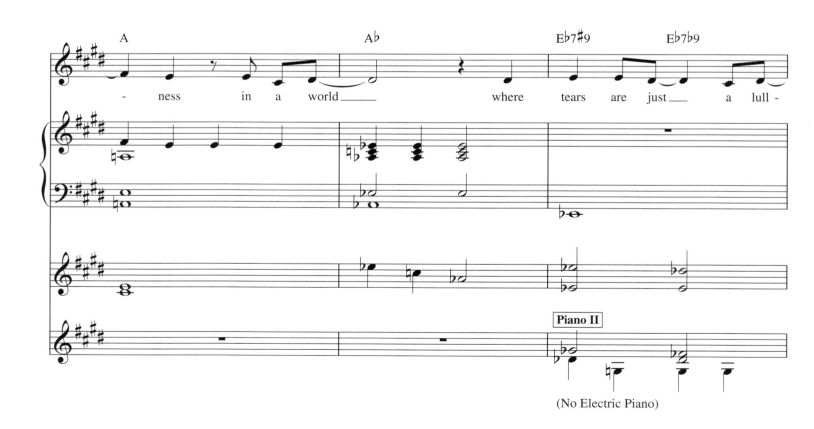

- ness in a world where tears are just a lull -

(No Electric Piano)

-ing with a smile on your face ___ and show the world ___ all ___

___ the love ___ in your heart. _____ Then

peo - ple gon - na treat you bet - ter. ___ You're gon - na find, yes ___ you will, ___

that you're beau - ti - ful, you're beau-

(Piano II)

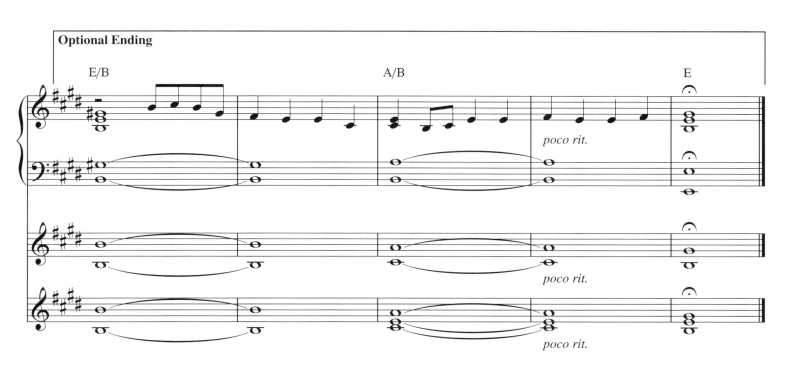

Been to Canaan

Words and Music by Carole King

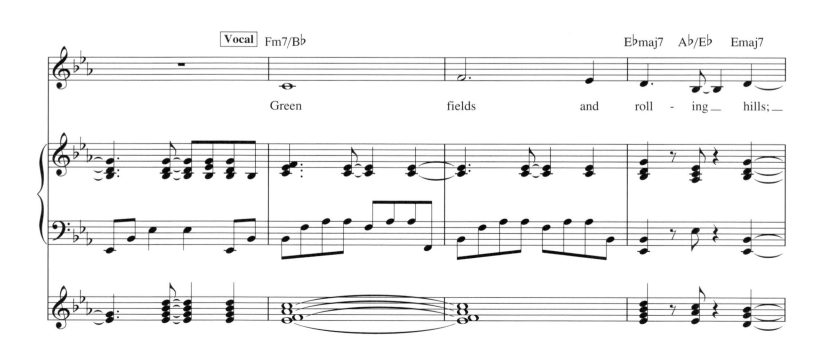

runnin' through__ my mind____ of a place__ I left__ be - hind.____

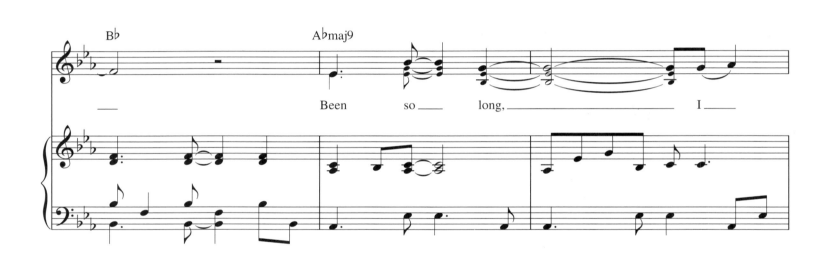

Been so__ long,_____ I

can't re - mem - ber__ when.__ I've been to Ca - naan and I

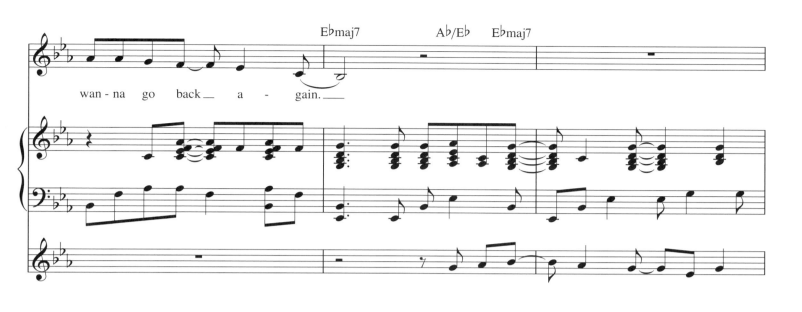

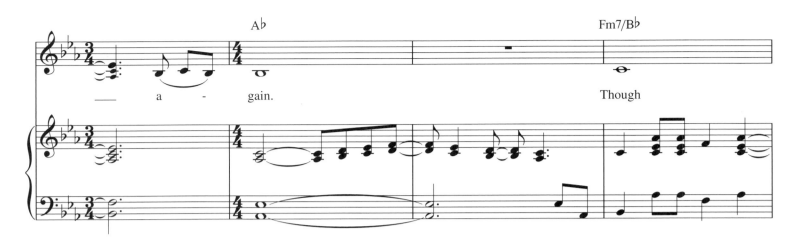

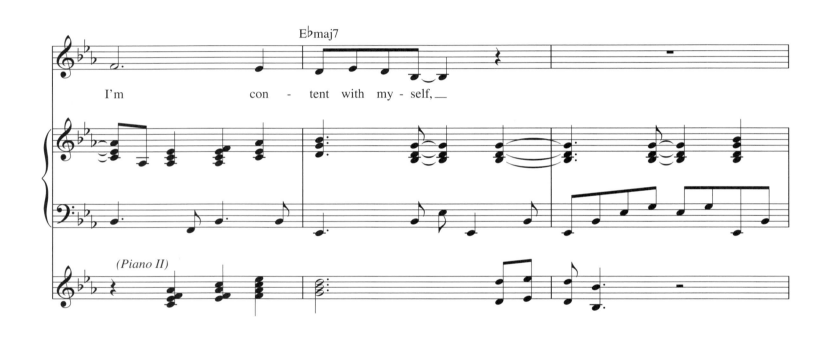

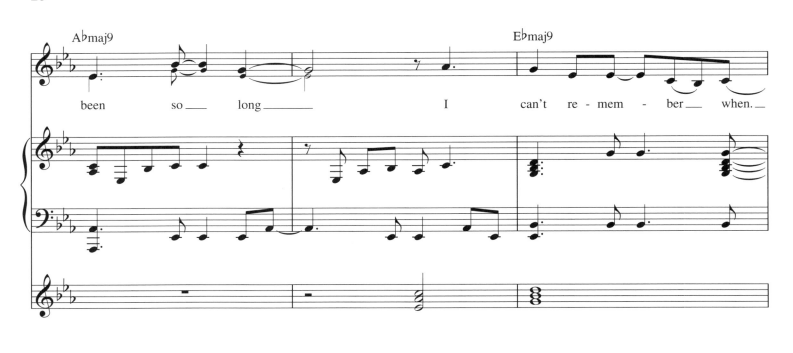

been so long I can't re-mem-ber when.

I've been to Ca-naan and I wan-na go back a-gain.

Been so long.

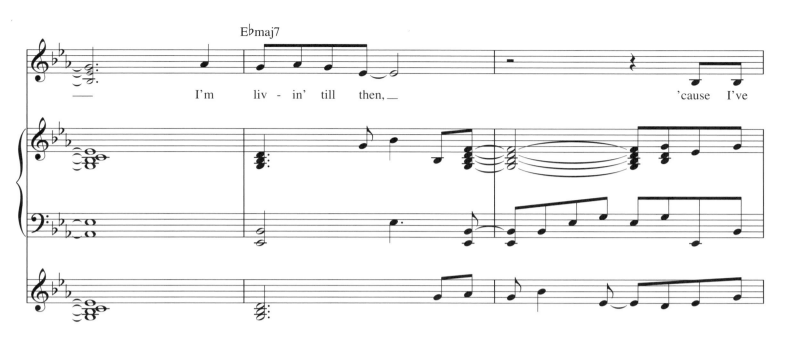

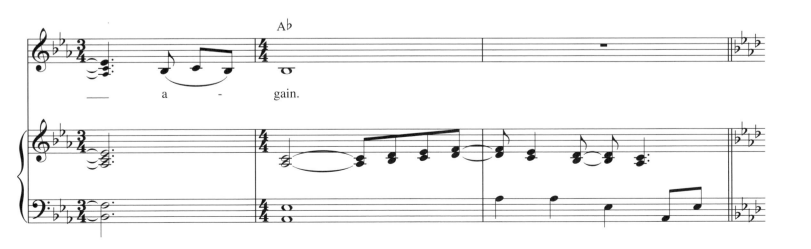

32

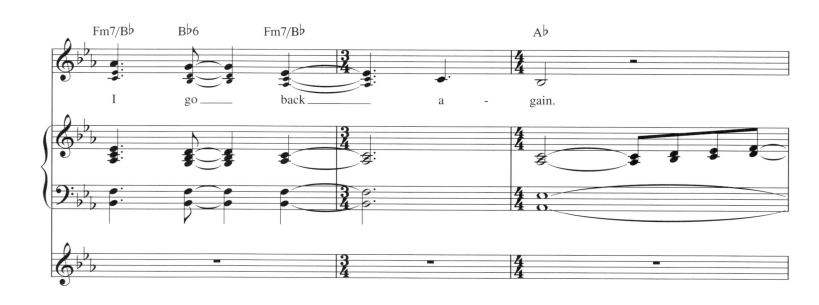

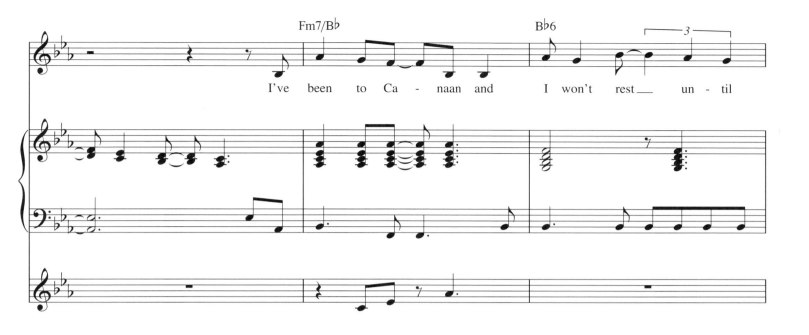

I've been to Ca - naan and I won't rest__ un - til

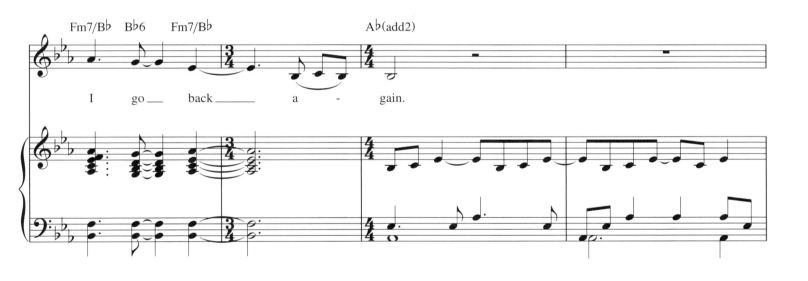

I go__ back__ a - gain.

Home Again

Words and Music by Carole King

Some-times I won-der if I'm ev-er gon-na make it home____ a-gain.____

It's so far____ and out of sight.

I real-ly need some-one to talk____ to, and no-bod-y else

I won't be hap-py till I ____ see ____ you ____ a - lone ____ a - gain, ____

till I'm home ____ a - gain ____ and feel - in' right. ____

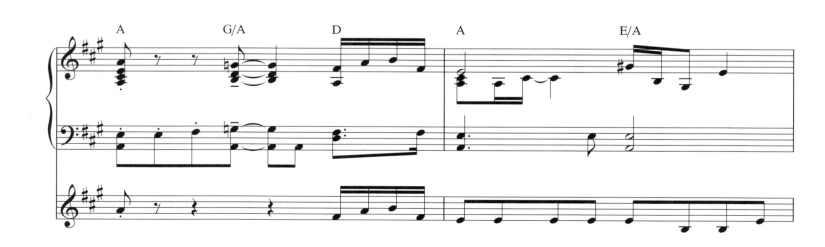

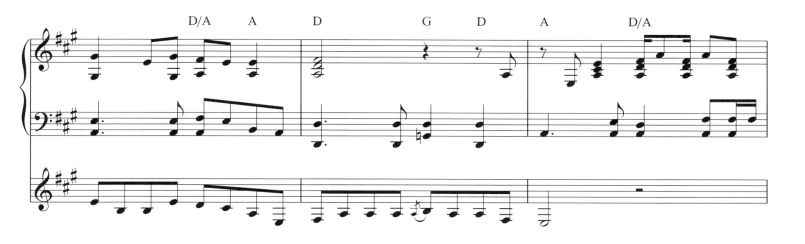

I Feel the Earth Move

Words and Music by Carole King

* *The original recording contains two separate piano parts. For this arrangement, they have been combined to be playable as a solo.*

42

It's Too Late

Words by Toni Stern
Music by Carole King

One of us __ is chang-in', or may-be we've just __ stopped _ try - in'. __
you look so __ un-hap - py and I feel _____ like a fool. _____

Play Fill (2nd time)

And it's too _____ late, ba - by, now __ it's too late, though we
And it's too _____ late, ba - by, now __ it's too late.

8va -

Fill

Doo doo doo doo doo doo doo doo ___ doo doo. ___

Doo doo doo doo doo doo doo doo. ___

Guitar solo - ad lib.

52

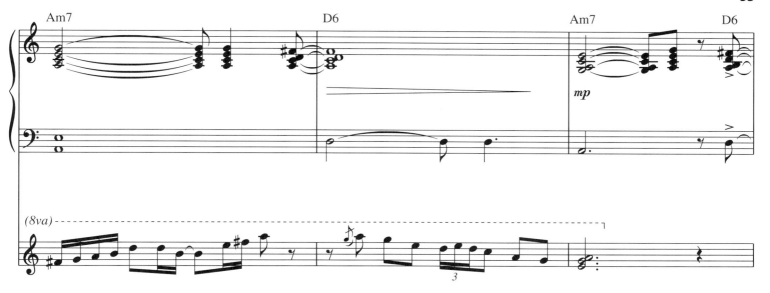

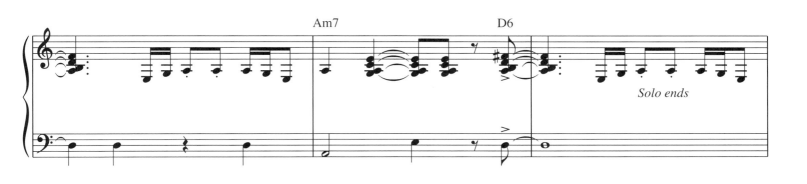

There'll be good times _ a - gain for me and _ you, _ but we just can't stay to-geth - er; don't _ you

it's too late, though we real-ly did ___ try to make ___ it.

it's too late, though we real-ly did ___ try to, we can't make ___ it now. ___

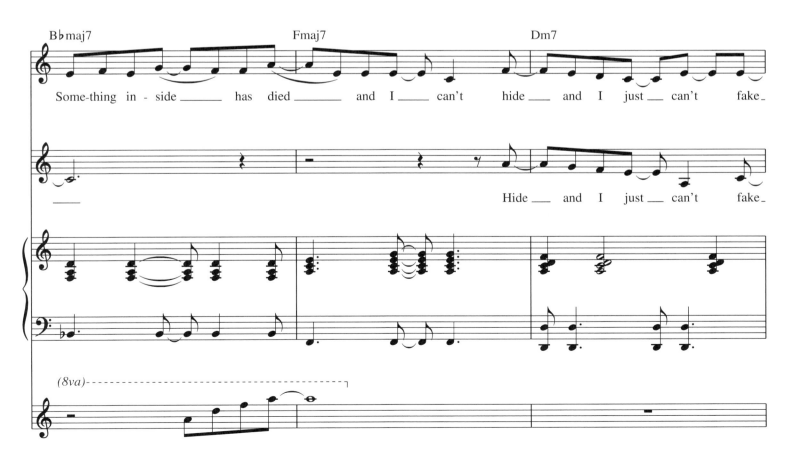

Some-thing in - side ___ has died ___ and I ___ can't hide ___ and I just ___ can't fake ___

___ Hide ___ and I just ___ can't fake ___

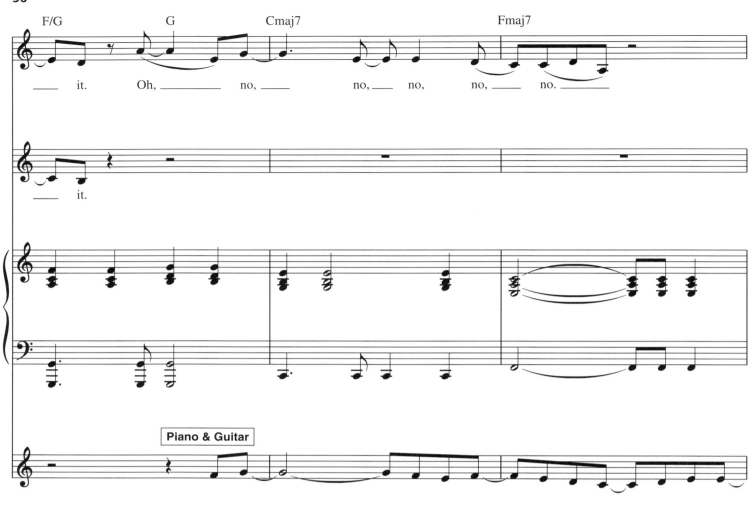

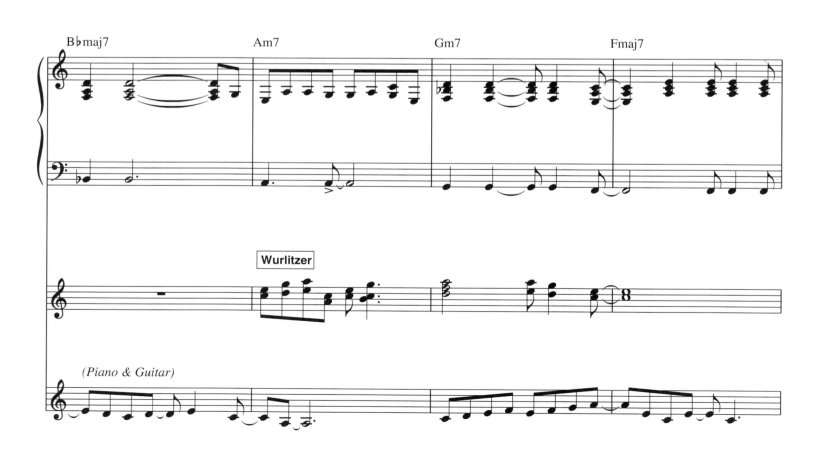

Jazzman

Words and Music by Carole King and David Palmer

Calmly ♩ = 120

Lift me, won't you lift me a-bove the old rou-

tine? Make it nice, play it clean, jazz-man.

cresc.

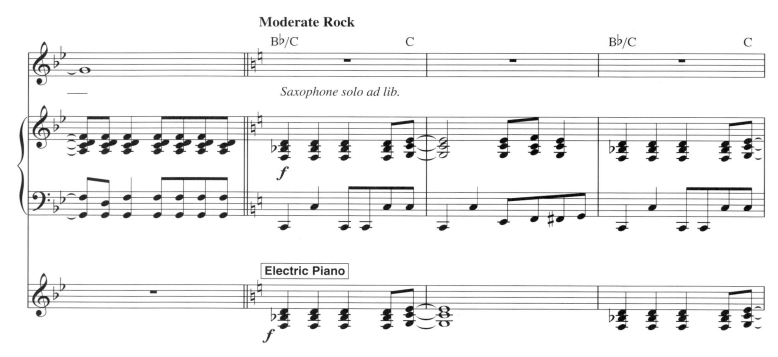

Moderate Rock

Saxophone solo ad lib.

Electric Piano

Jazz - man, _____ oh, jazz - man. _____

Saxophone Solo ad lib.

Solo ends When the

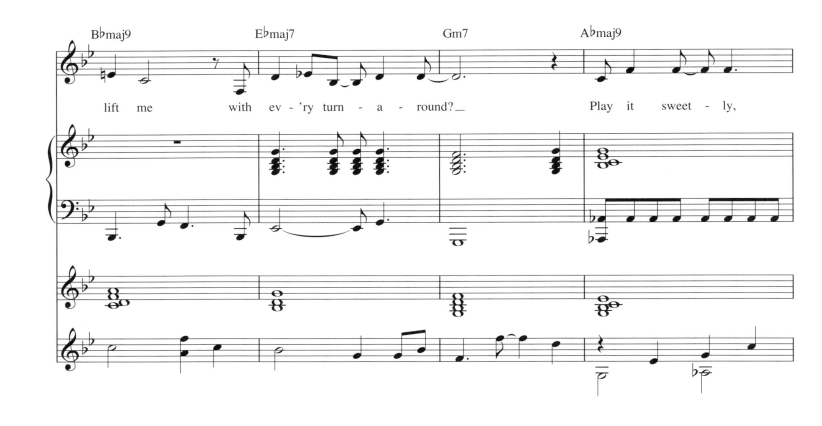

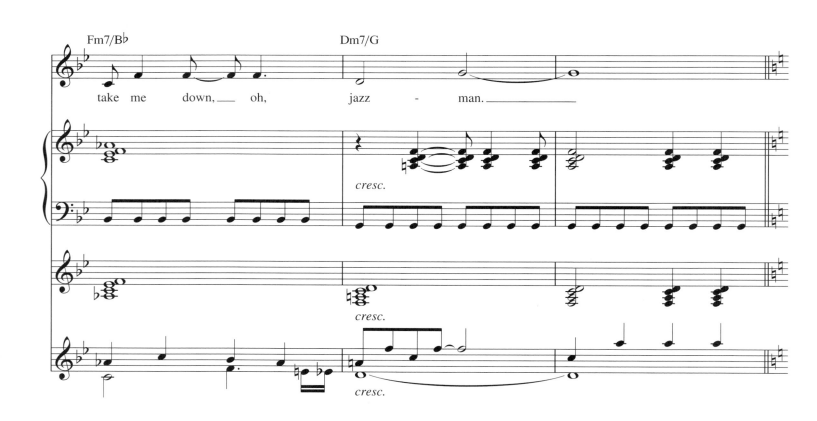

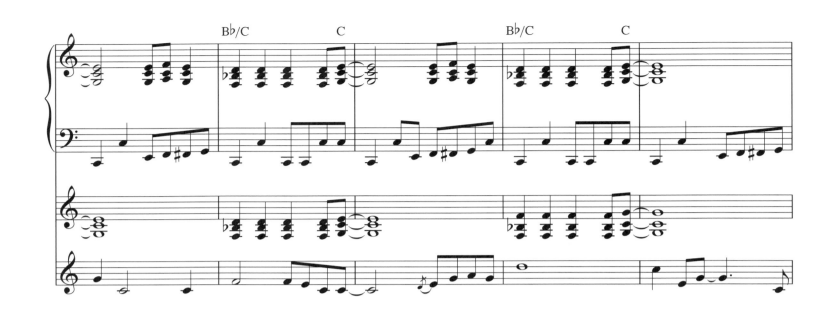

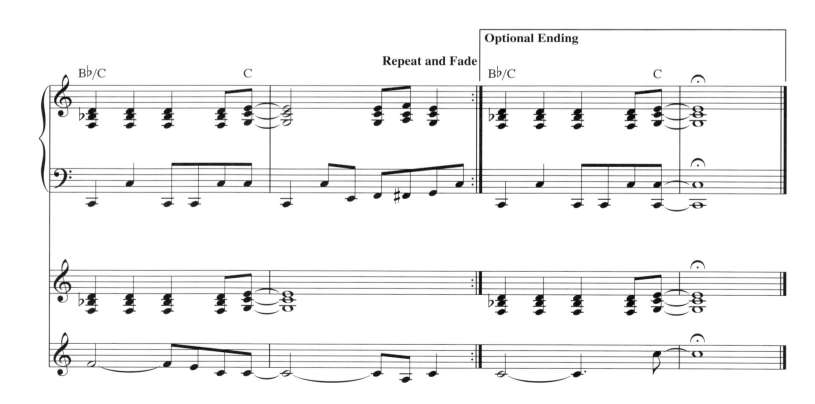

Smackwater Jack

Words and Music by Gerry Goffin and Carole King

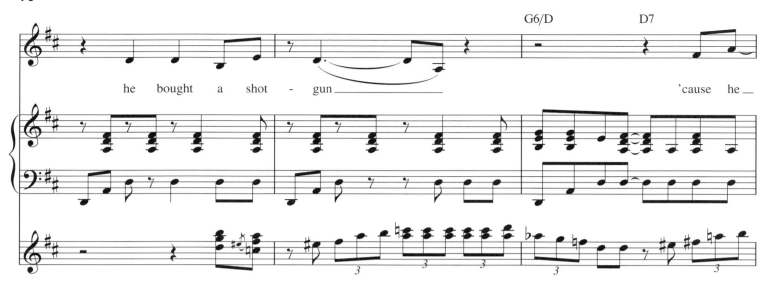

he bought a shot - gun _____ 'cause he __

_____ was in the mood for a lit - tle __ con - fron - ta - tion.

He just __ let it all __ hang loose; __ he did - n't

Oh,___ no,____ no,___ no,_____ no.

Ooh!

Guitar solo

8va

(8va)

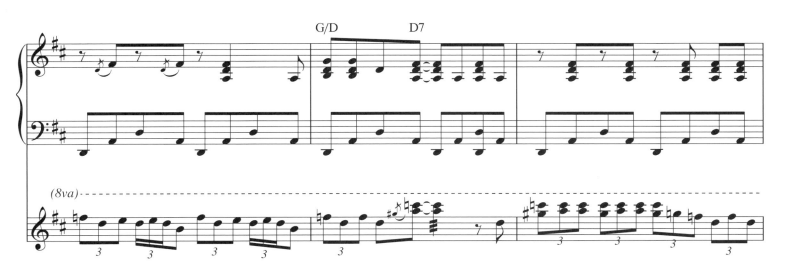

(8va)

Ooh, _____ talk - in' 'bout Jack and his shot -

- gun. Talk - in' 'bout Smack,_

talk - in' 'bout Jack,_ Smack - wa - ter Jack, yeah.

(You Make Me Feel Like)
A Natural Woman

Words and Music by Gerry Goffin, Carole King and Jerry Wexler

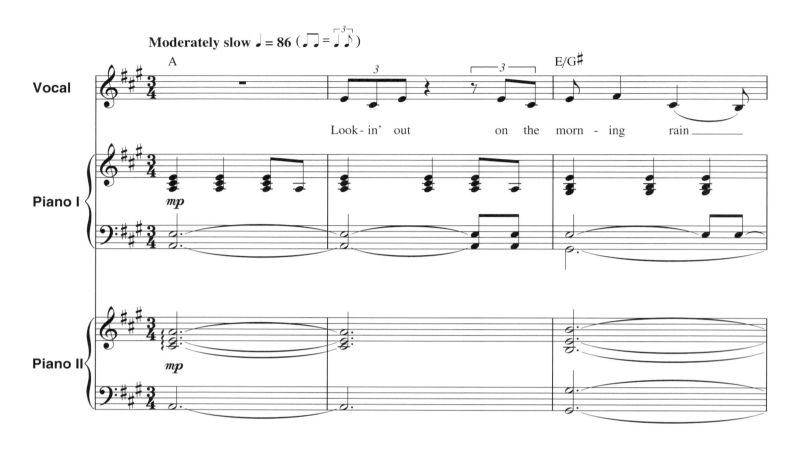

Look-in' out on the morn-ing rain

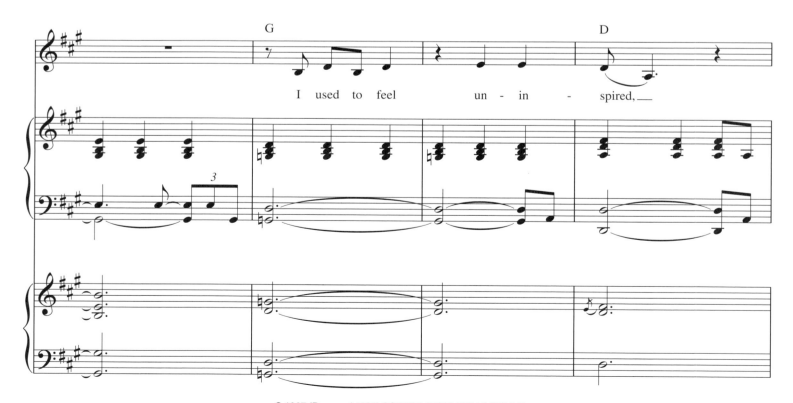

I used to feel un-in-spired,

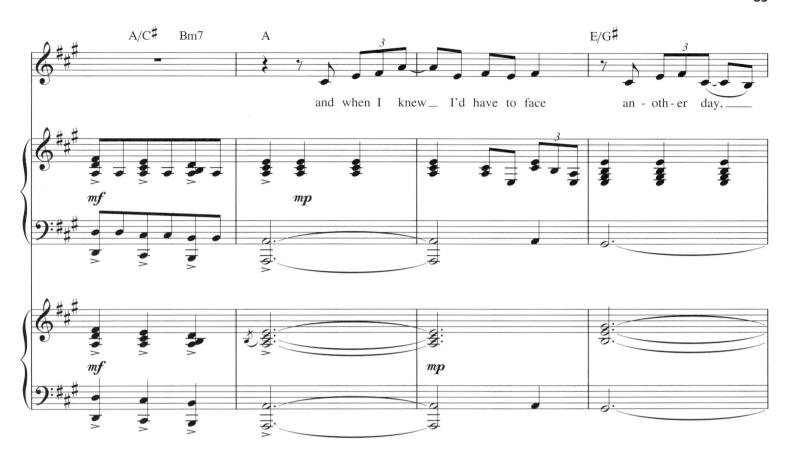

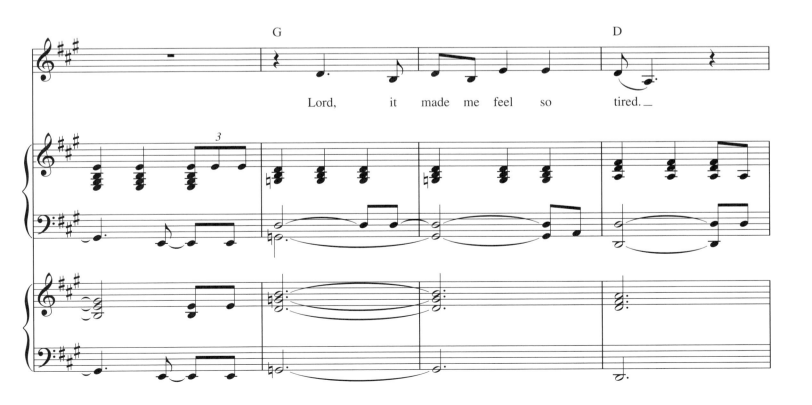

84

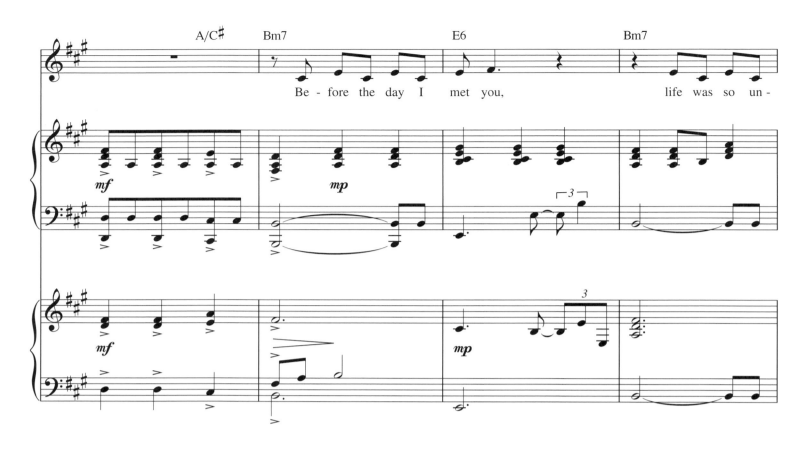

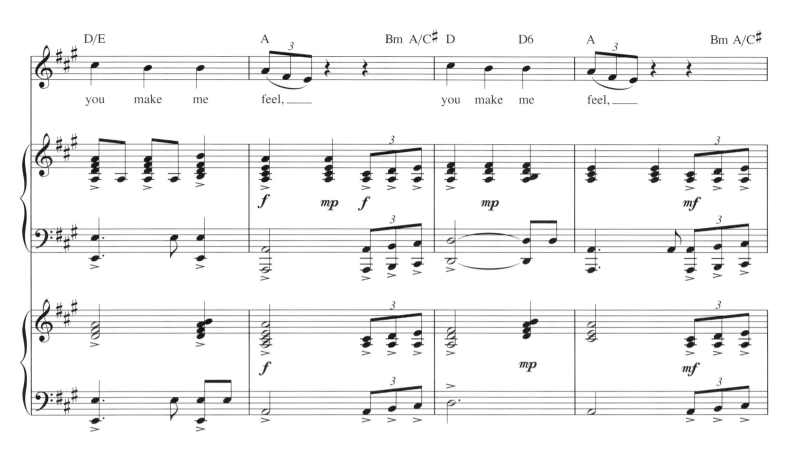

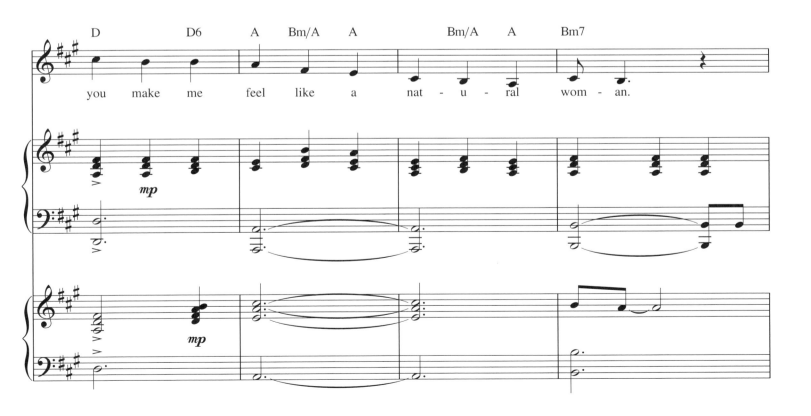

When my soul was in the lost and found, ___

you came ___ a - long to claim it.

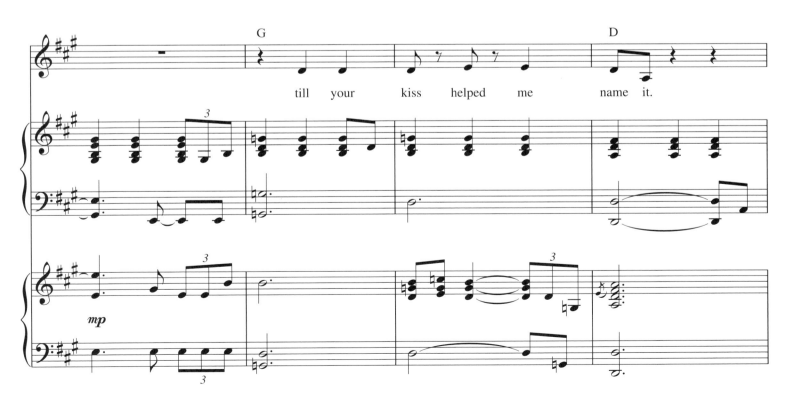

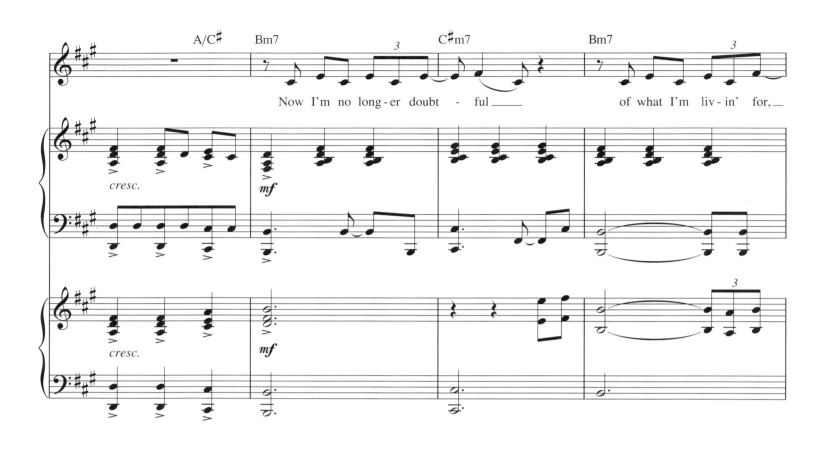

Now I'm no long-er doubt - ful_____ of what I'm liv-in' for, __

__ 'cause if I make you hap - py, I don't need to do __ more. _____

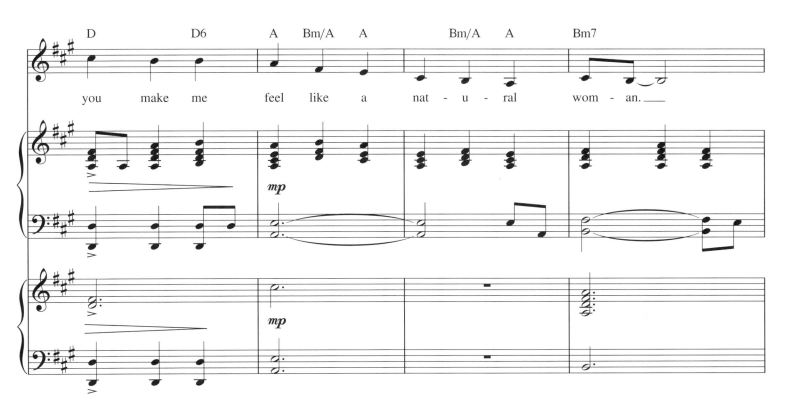

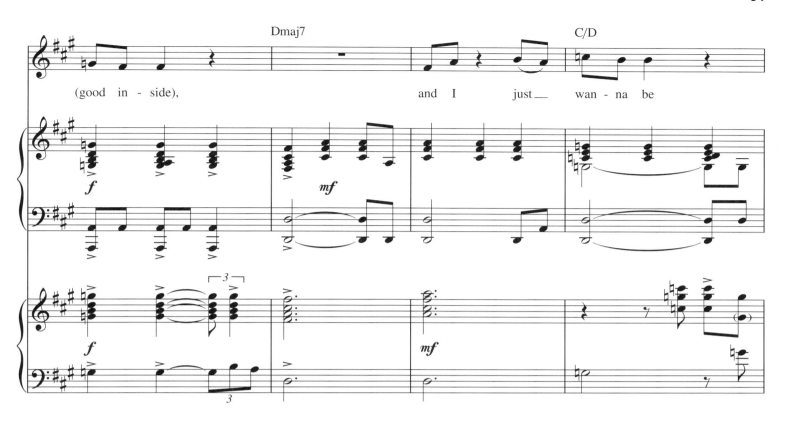

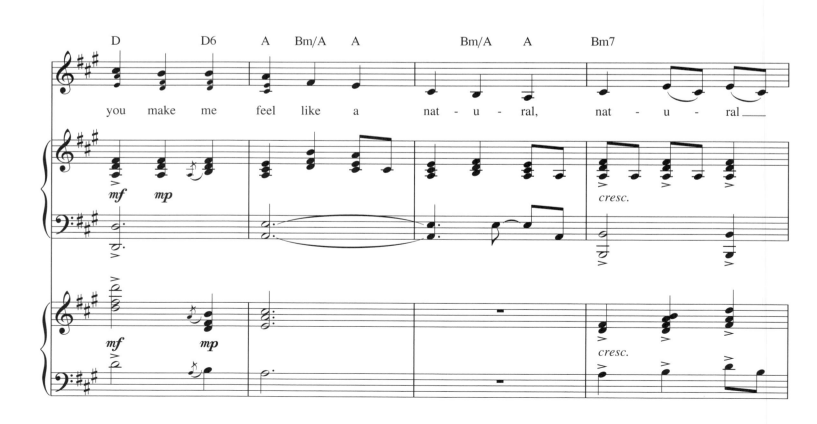

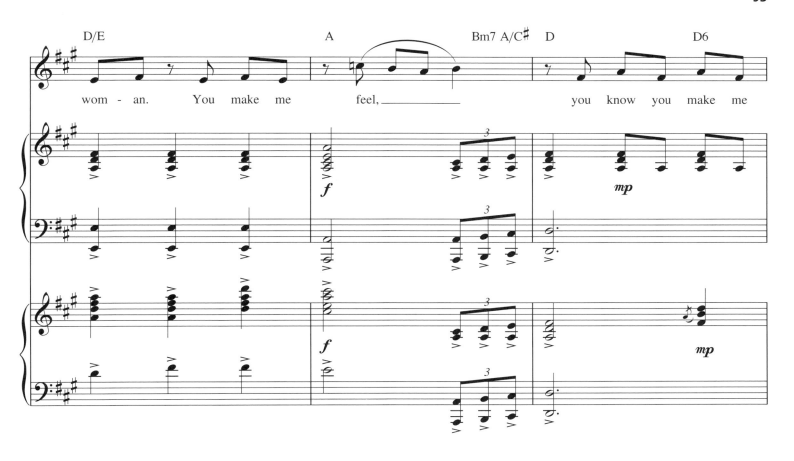

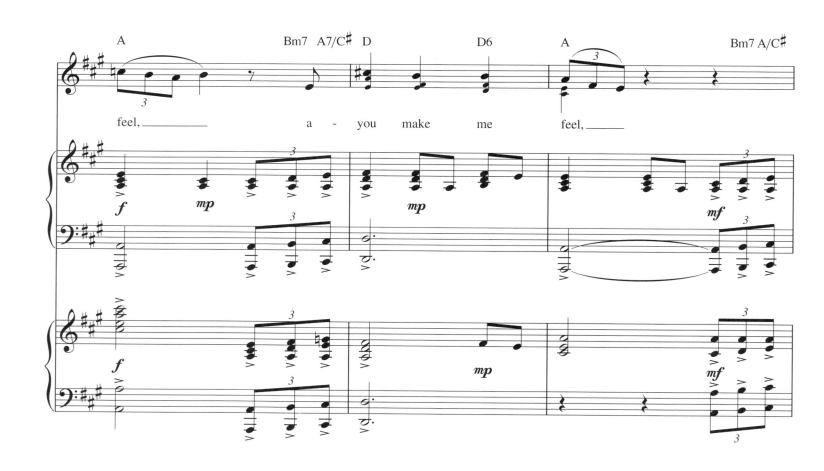

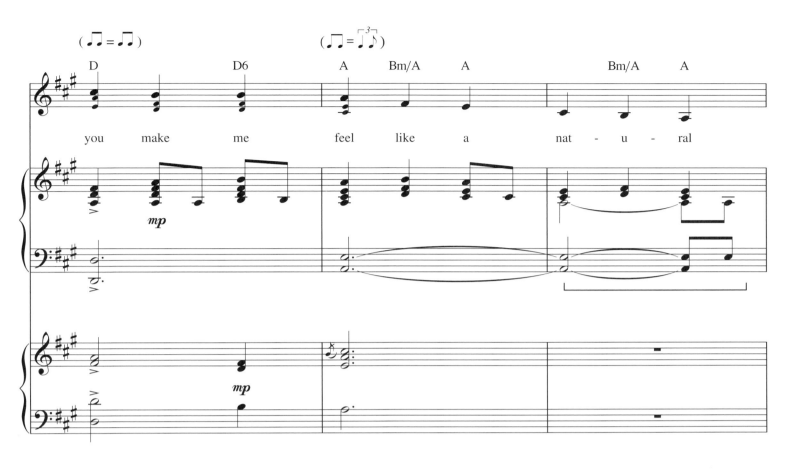

you make me feel like a nat - u - ral

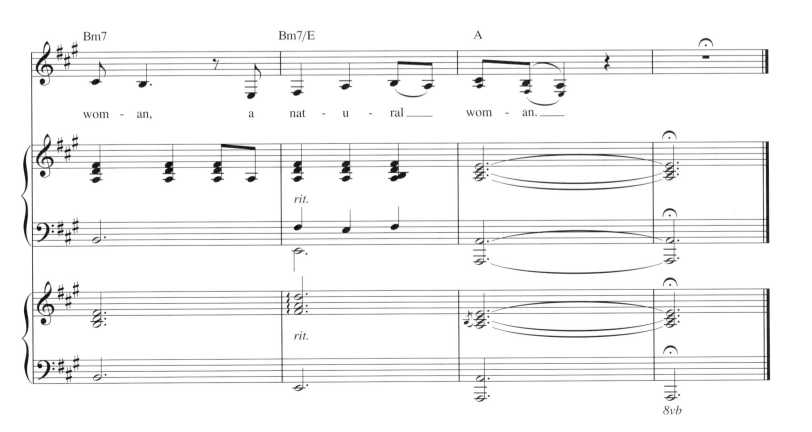

wom - an, a nat - u - ral____ wom - an.____

Nightingale

Words and Music by Carole King and David Palmer

This arrangement combines the two piano tracks to make them playable by one pianist.

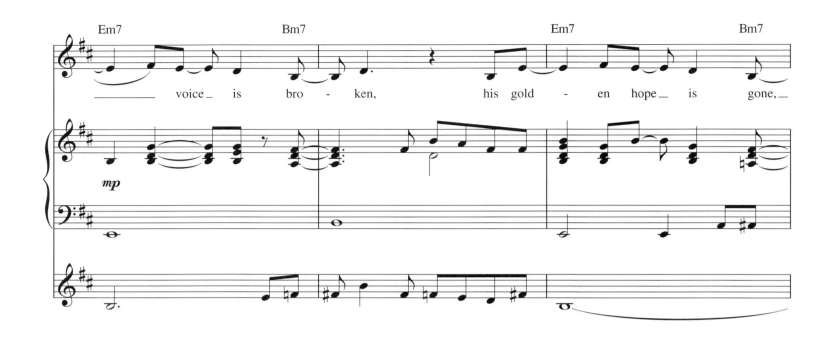

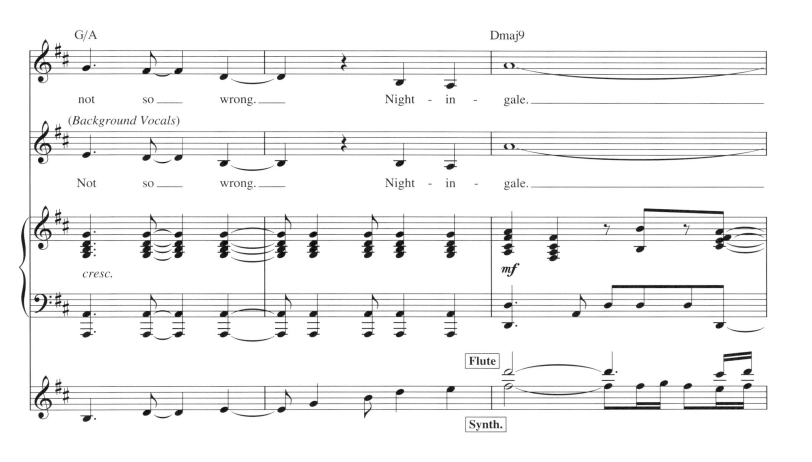

Gmaj9

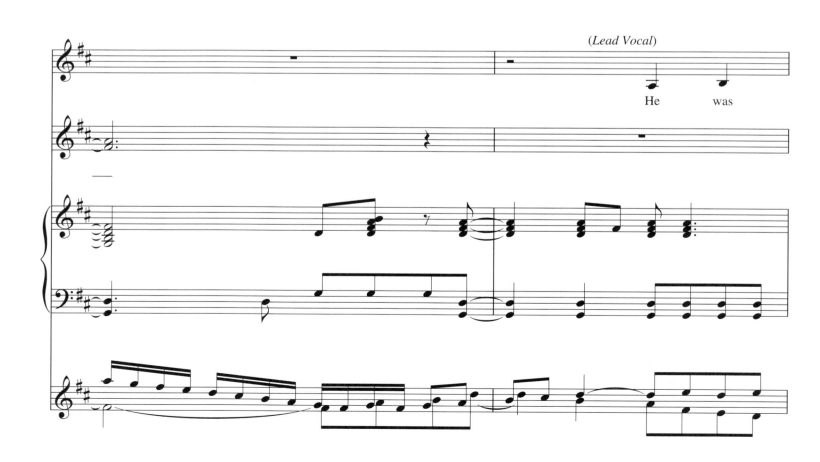

(*Lead Vocal*)

He   was

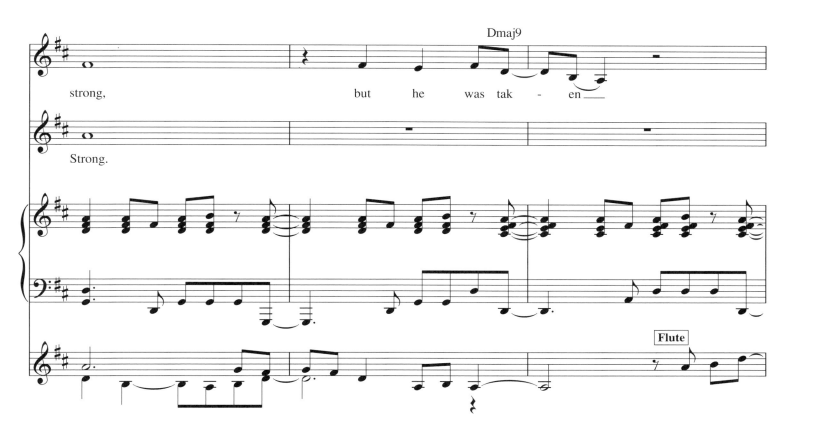

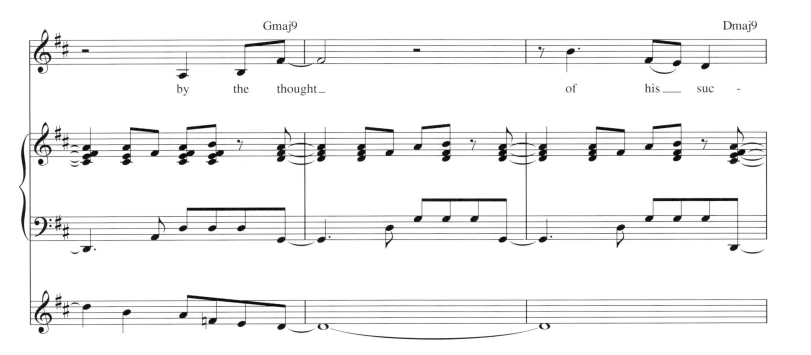

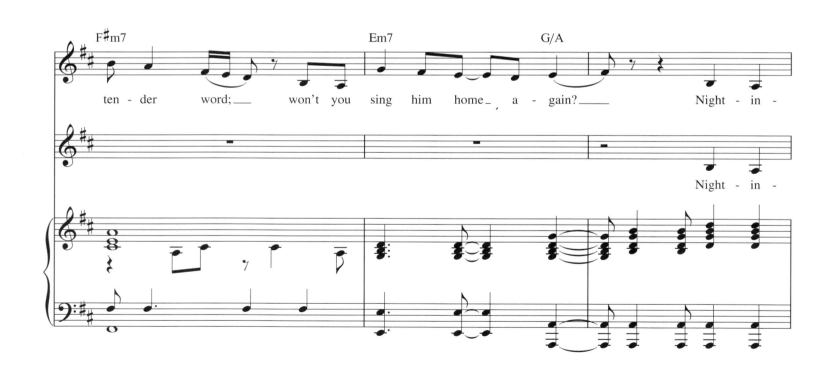

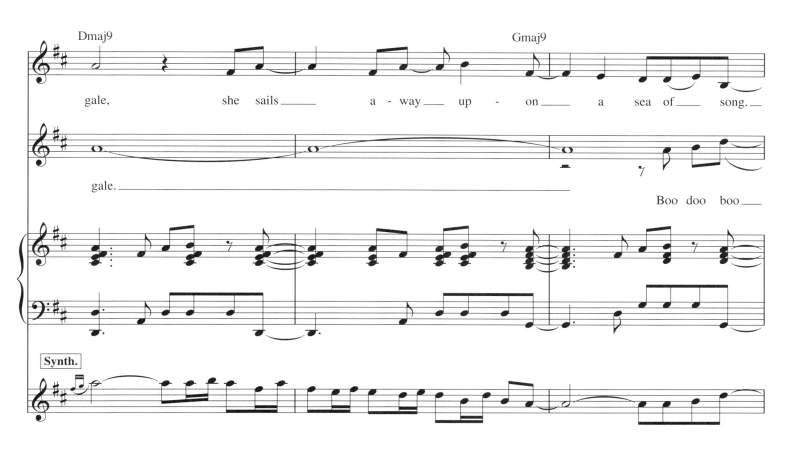

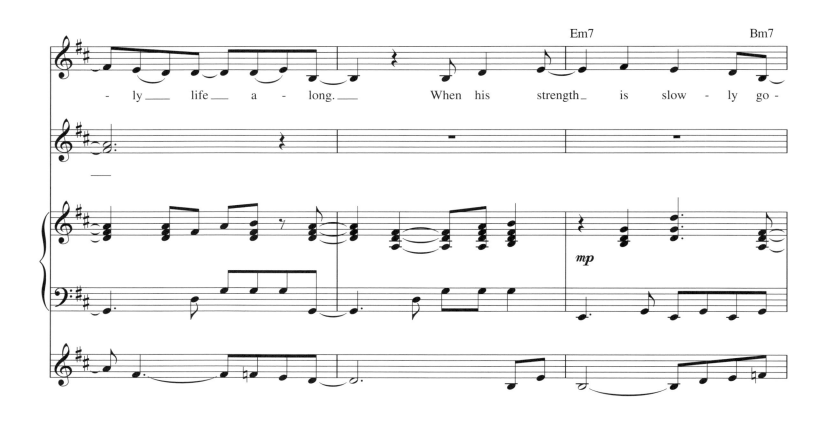

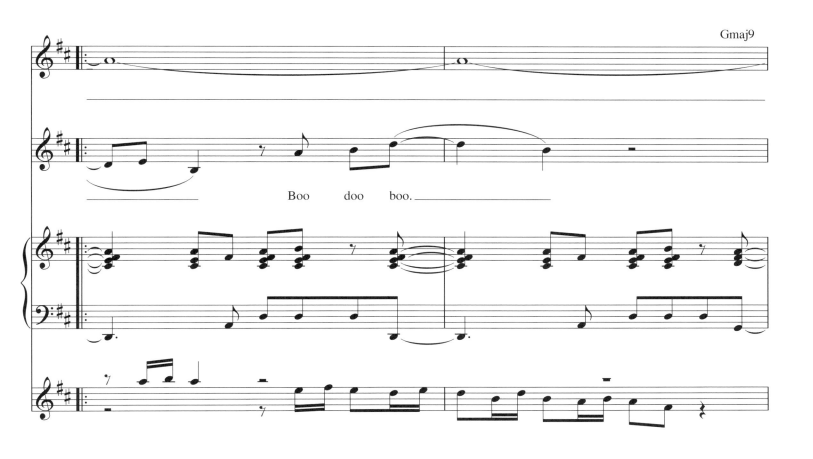

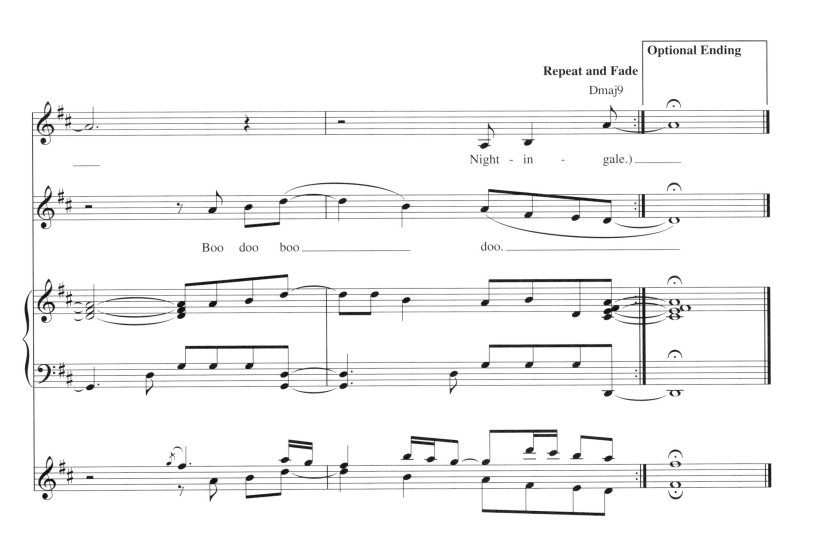

So Far Away

Words and Music by Carole King

rath - er spend __ it be - in' close to you, but you're so

far a - way! __

far a - way! __

Doesn't an - y - bod - y stay in one place __

Doesn't an - y - bod - y stay in one place __

Play Fill (2nd time)

__ an - y - more?

__ an - y - more? __

It would be so fine to see __ your __

It would be so fine __ to see __ your

Fill

mp

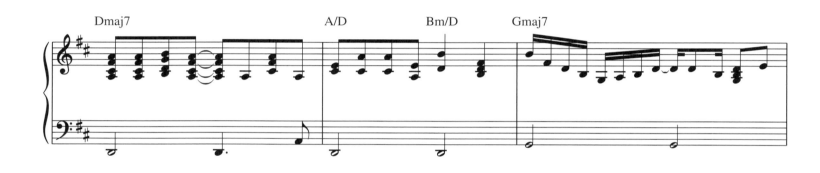

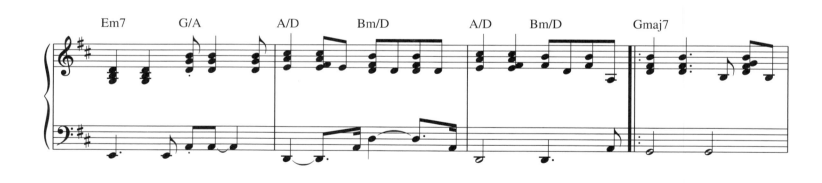

Repeat ad lib. and Fade | **Optional Ending**

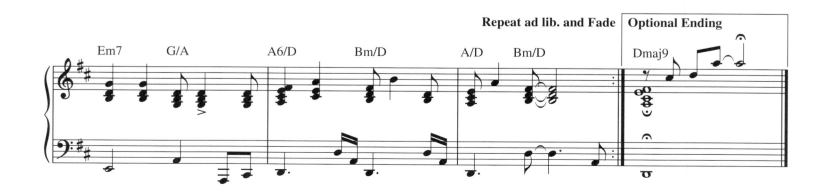

Sweet Seasons

Words and Music by Carole King and Toni Stern

Some - times you win, some - times you lose, and some - times the blues get a hold of you, oh, just when you thought you had made it.

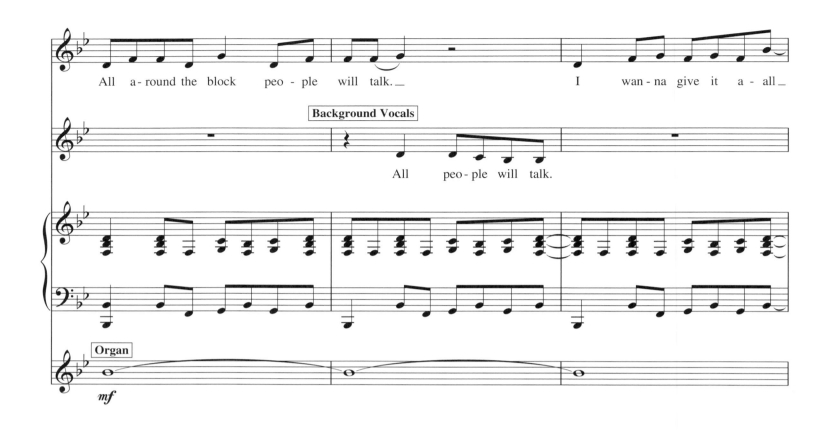

All a-round the block peo-ple will talk. __ I wan-na give it a-all __

Background Vocals

All peo-ple will talk.

Organ

mf

__ that I got; I __ just don't __ want, I don't __ wan-na waste __

Cm7/F

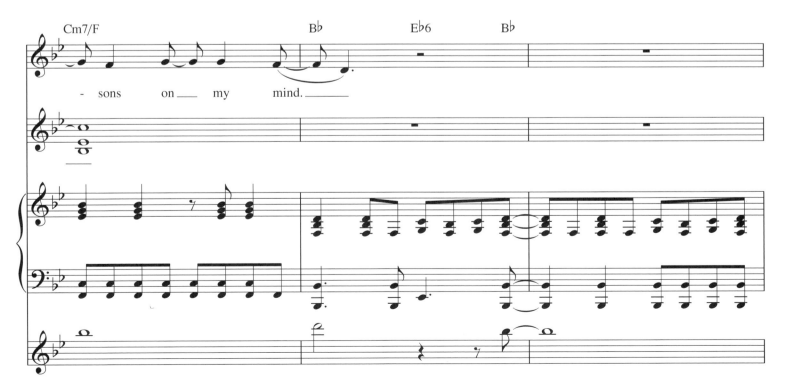

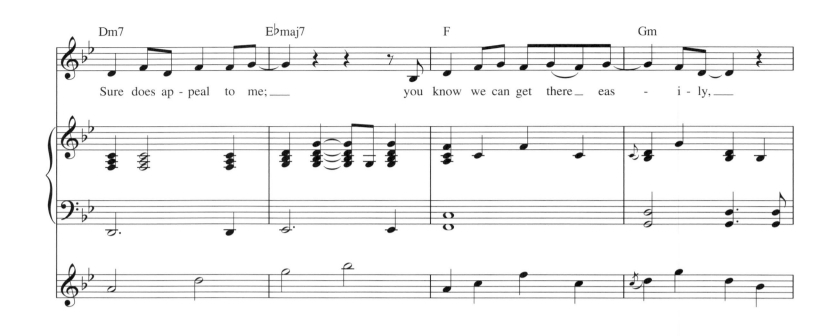

Sure does ap - peal to me; ___ you know we can get there ___ eas - i - ly, ___

just like a sail - boat sail - ing on ___ the ___ sea. ___

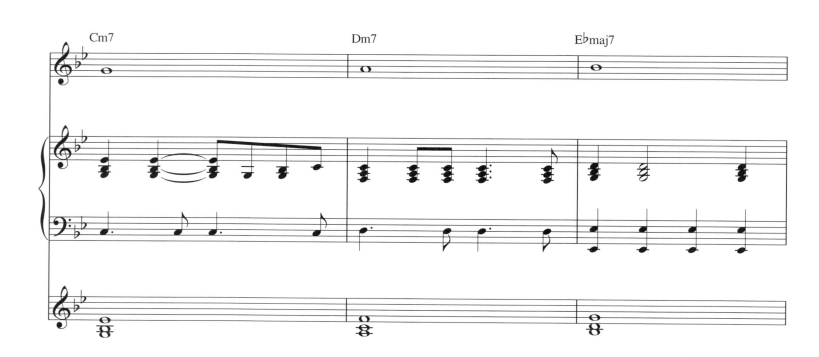

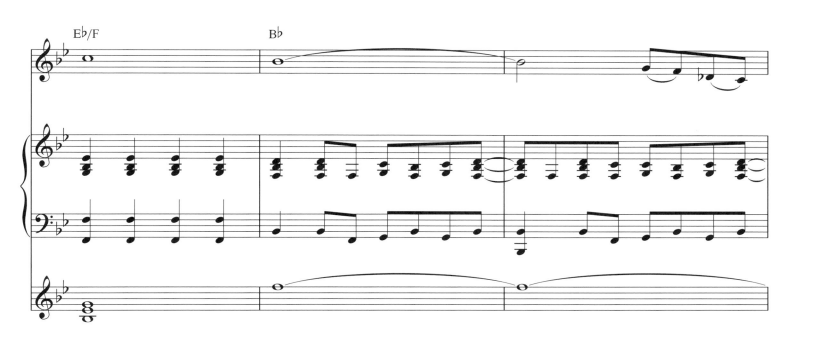

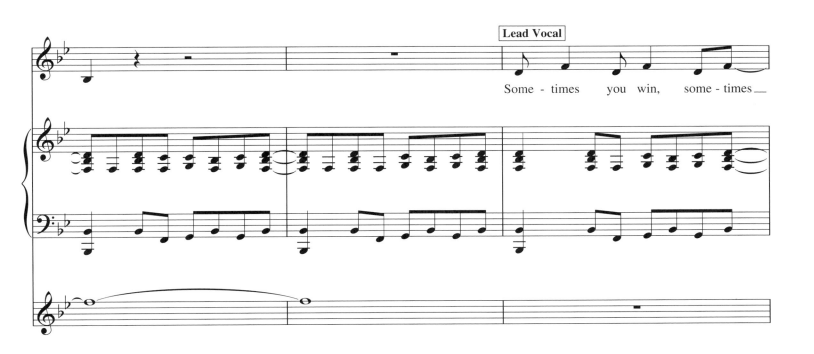

Some - times   you win,   some - times____

But I'll have some kids and make my plan, and

I'll watch the sea - sons run-nin' a - way,__ and I'll build__ me a life__ in the o-

128

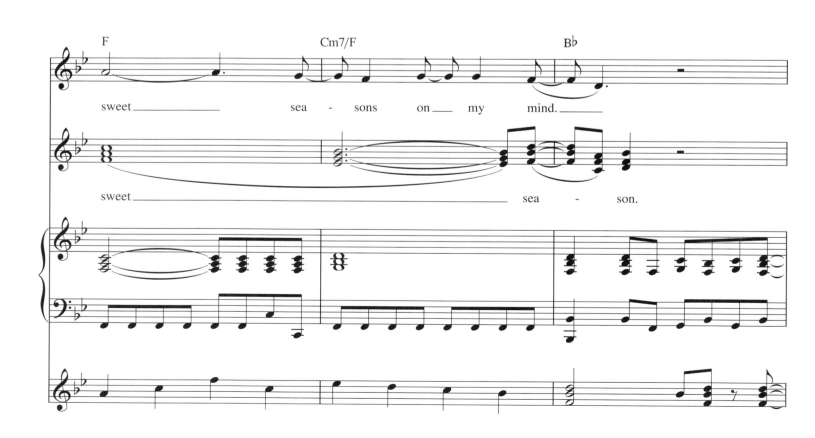

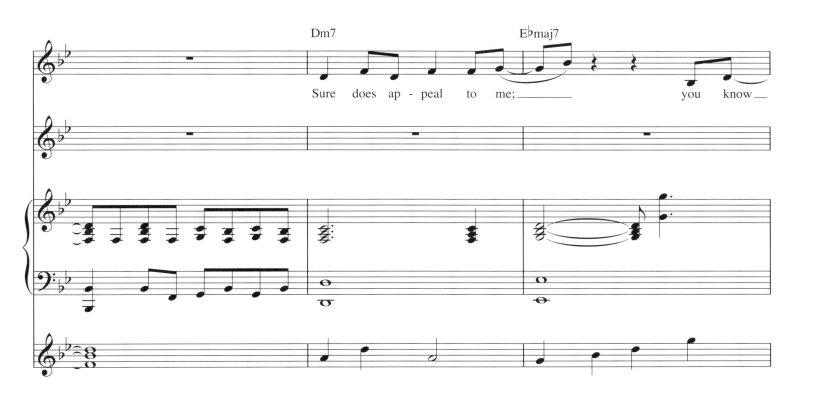

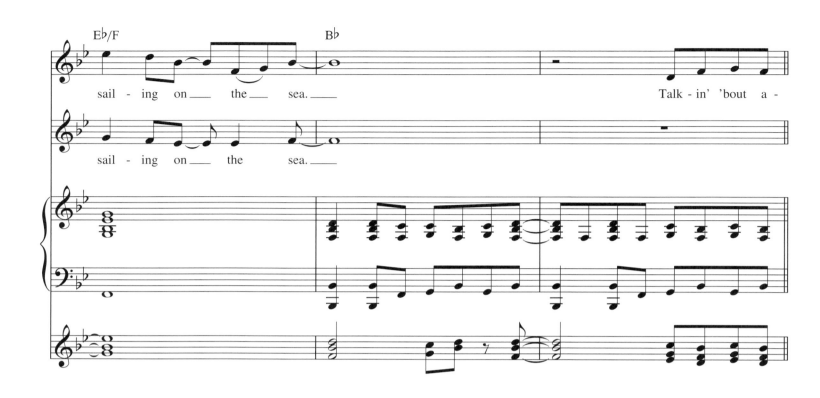

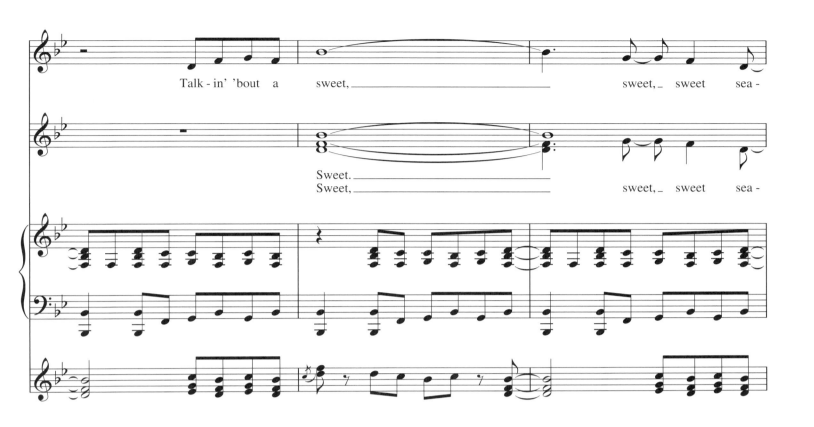

Tapestry

Words and Music by Carole King

The original recording contains two separate piano parts. For this arrangement, they have been combined to be playable as a solo.

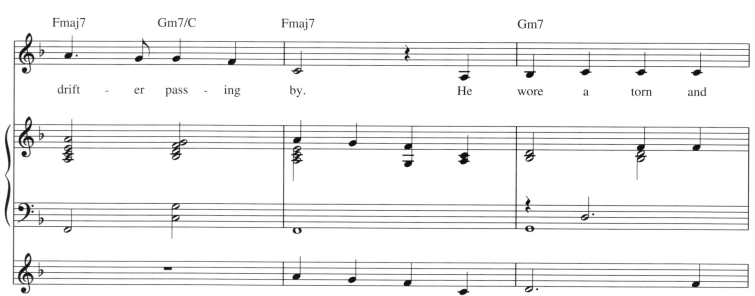

136

138

Way Over Yonder

Words and Music by Carole King

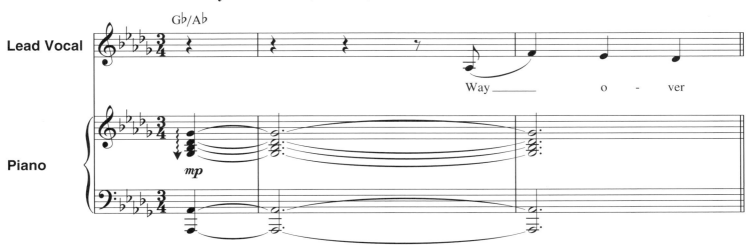

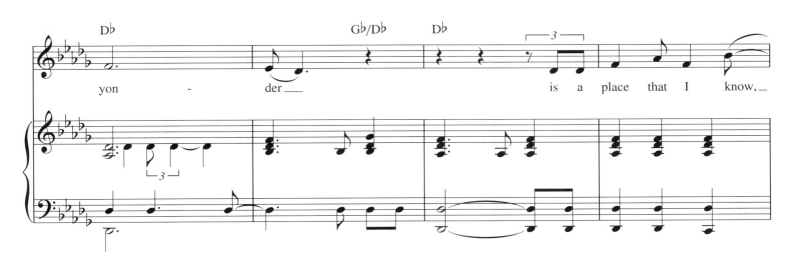

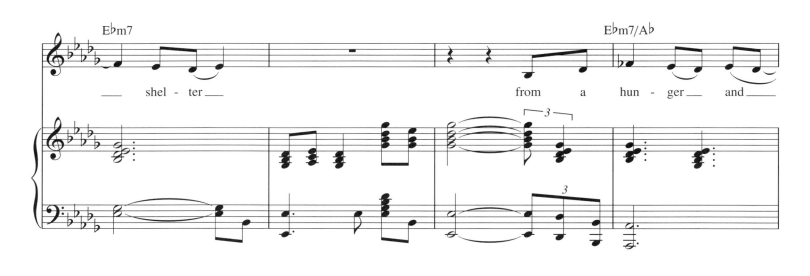

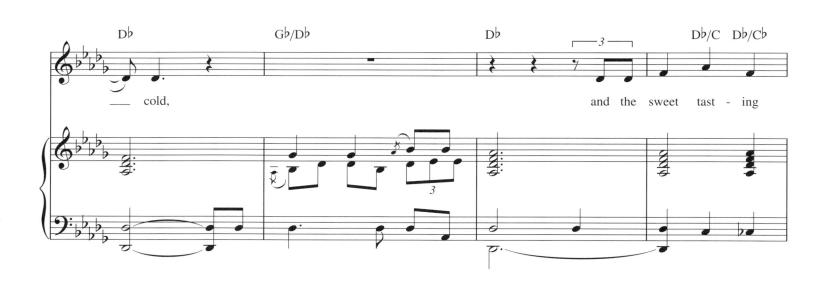

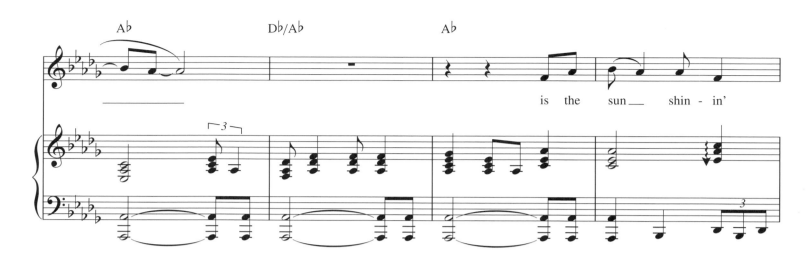

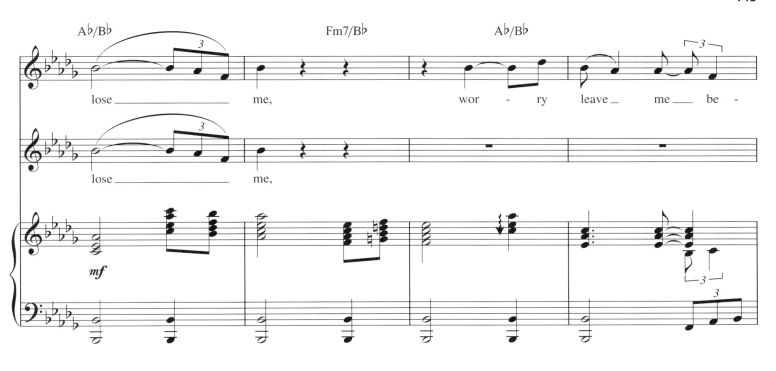

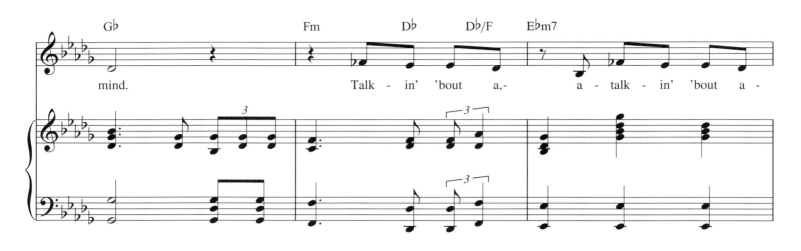

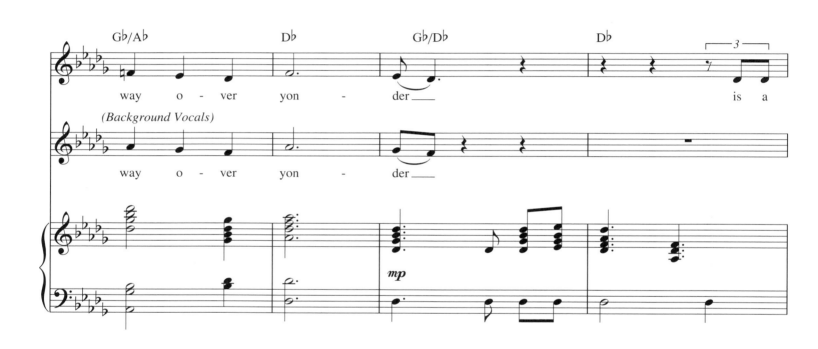

I'll find my way_____ to the

(Background Vocals)
I'll find my___ way.____

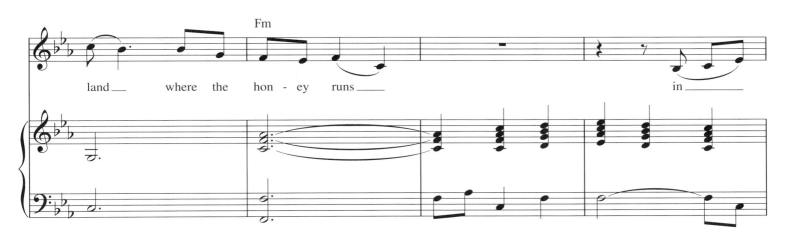

land___ where the hon - ey runs_____ in ____

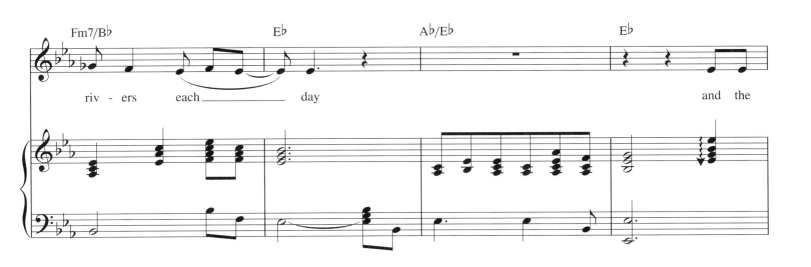

riv - ers each_____ day and the

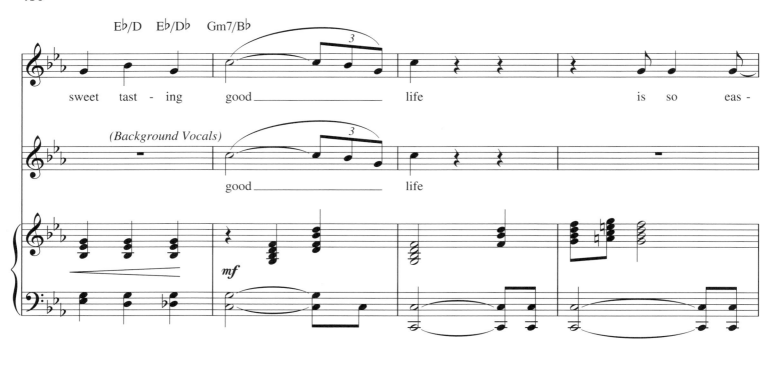

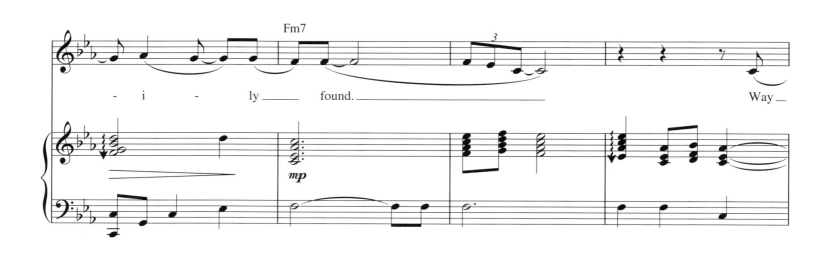

Where You Lead

Words and Music by Carole King and Toni Stern

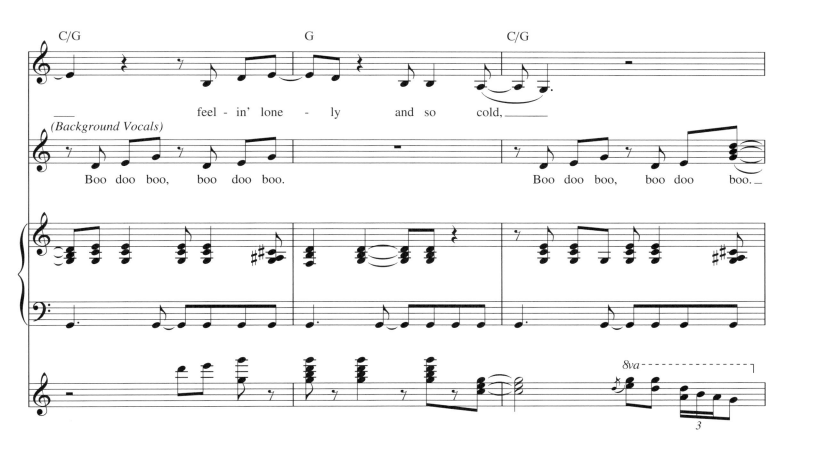

158

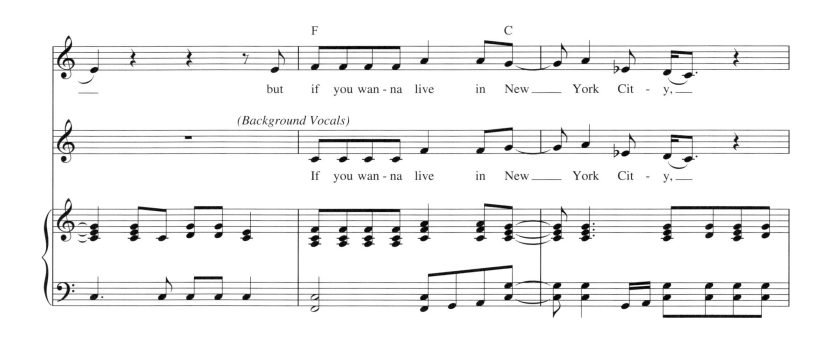

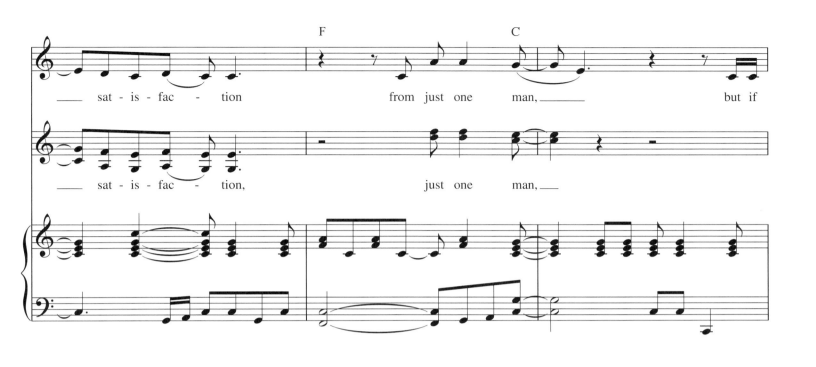

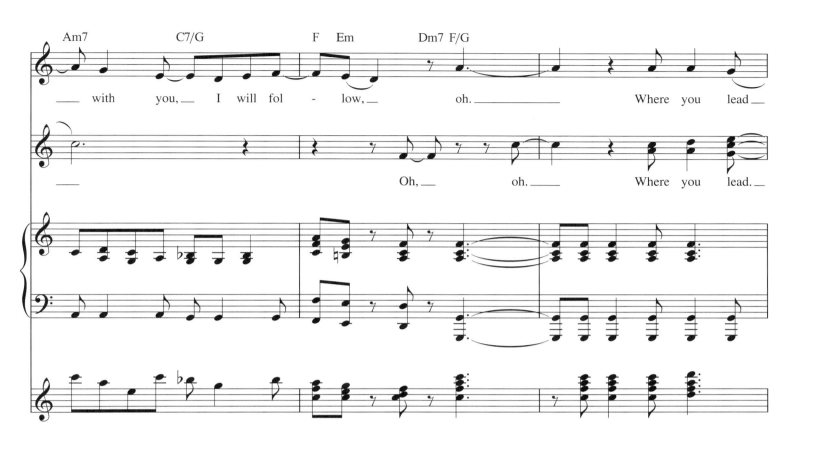

- by, yeah.___ I'm gon - na fol - low where___ you lead._____

___ you lead.___

Ooh, yeah, ba - by.

I'm gon - na fol - low where___ you lead._____

Optional Ending

Will You Love Me Tomorrow
(Will You Still Love Me Tomorrow)

Words and Music by Gerry Goffin and Carole King

* Recording begins at ♩ = 69 and accelerates during verse 1 to ♩ = 80.

Top bkg. vocal note written one octave higher than sung throughout.

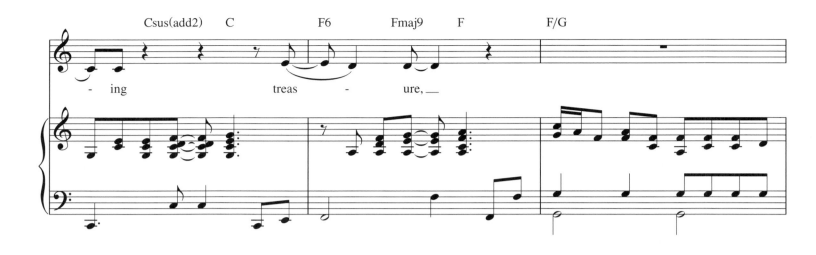

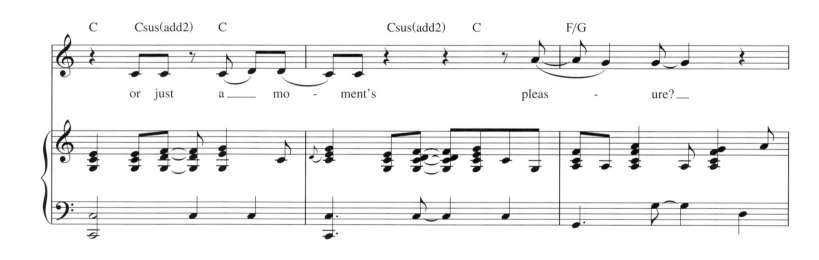

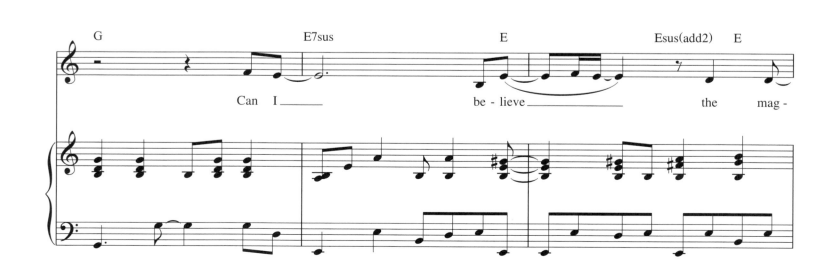

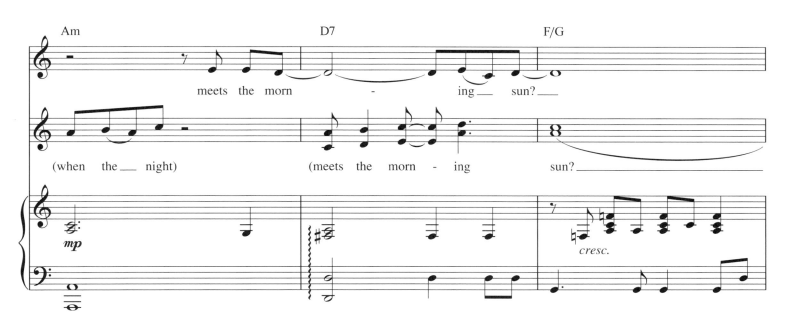

meets the morn - ing __ sun?__

(when the __ night) (meets the morn - ing sun?_____)

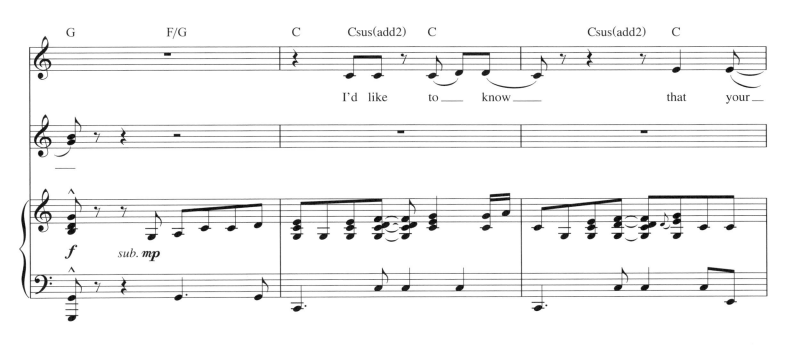

I'd like to __ know __ that your __

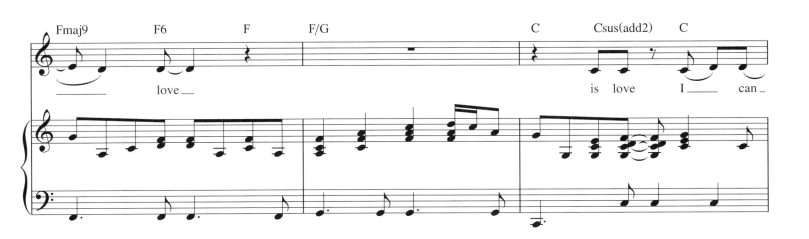

__ love __ is love I __ can __

172

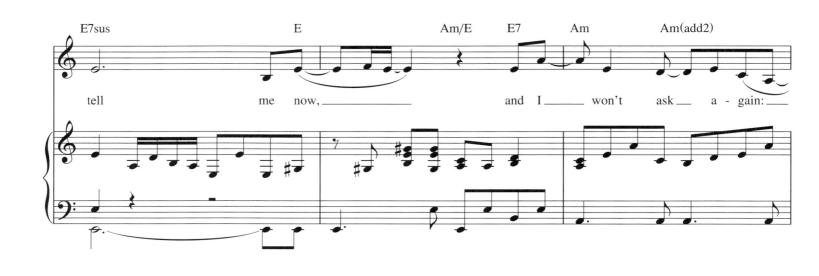

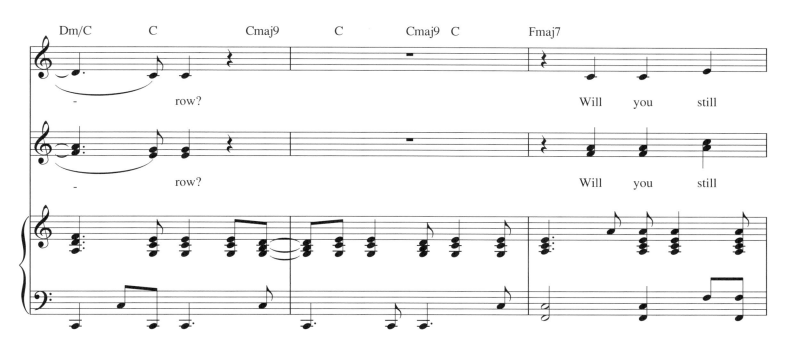

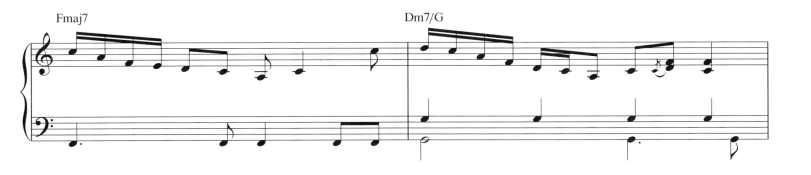

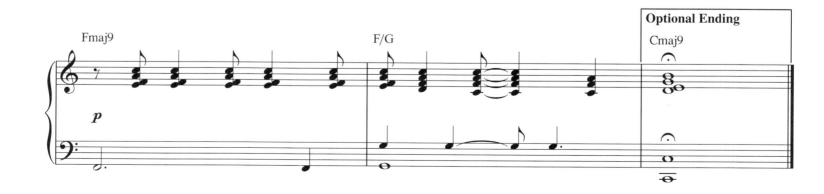

You've Got a Friend

Words and Music by Carole King

(Play L.H. in octaves 2nd time)

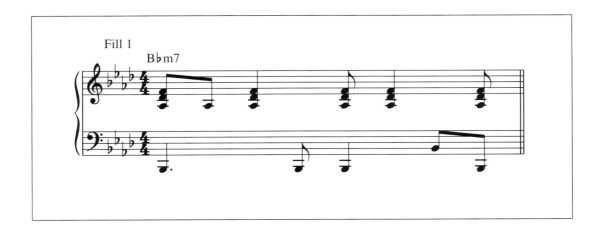

Fill 2 (Vocal)

I'll come run - nin', ___ run-nin', yeah, yeah, ___ to see you a - gain.
(I'll come run - nin', ___ yeah.) ___